"...Cribbs' eloquent command of time and place puts the reader squarely into his mind's eye..."
Halifax Magazine

"...Randy Cribbs is vibrantly alive inside each of his books..."
Flagler Magazine

"...Cribbs is becoming quite a prolific writer..."
St. Augustine Record

"I've never read anything quite so original and would recommend it as a good read."
Peter Guinta, Senior Writer,
St. Augustine Record

". . . his passion for the area's history, architecture and colorful characters-past and present- provides endless inspiration. . .such a craftsman and really works hard at getting it clean and clear for the reader. . . with Randy, it is all about vision..."
The St. Johns Sun

Ancient City Treasures

Copyright © 2006 by Randy Cribbs

Cover design by Jennifer Ricker, LeftEar Design.
Interior layout by Matt Cribbs, LeftEar Design.
www.lefteardesign.com

All rights reserved. No part of this book may be reproduced, stored in a retrieval system or transmitted in any form, electronic, mechanical, or by other means, without written permission of the author.

Published by OCRS, Inc.
P.O. Box 551627
Jacksonville, FL 32255

Library of Congress
Control Number: 2006905820

ISBN 0-9725796-5-6
ISBN 13: 978-0-9725796-5-0

Printed in the United States of America
For more information, go to
www.somestillserve.com

A Special Gift

For:
_____

From:
_____

Date:
_____

Dedicated to
AnnaJane, Eilis, and Leah

Ancient City Treasures

By
Randy Cribbs

The author gratefully acknowledges the St. Augustine Historical Society Research Library for the 1880's Heppenheimer and Maurer front cover lithograph and the historical E.A. Meyer drawings shown in "Ancient City Treasures". A special thanks to library director Charles Tingley and his staff.

Author's Note

After thirty plus world traveling years, the special feeling I have for St. Augustine has not diminished. The excitement and fascination I felt walking her streets as a young boy is still in me, and, I hope, in the books I've written with the Old Town as centerpiece. In **'Ancient City Treasures'**, I wanted to take you on a tour from the heart through the town's rich history and mystique. The wonderful turn of the century drawings by E. A. Meyer very much capture the feel of the Old Town I wanted to share, and I hope you will share with others. Let the Ancient City spirit enter you as it has me.

Also by Randy Cribbs
The Vessel
Tales from the Oldest City
One Summer in the Old Town
Illumination Rounds
Were You There

Table of Contents
Ancient Places

Welcome	1
Ancient City	3
Aviles Street	5
Tolomato	7
Oldest Drugstore	9
Old Jail	11
Old Town Streets	13
Castillo de San Marcos	15
Lighthouse Porch	17
Oldest House	19
Lasting	21
Plaza Beginning	23
Renovation	25
Oldest Schoolhouse	27
Fountain of Youth	29
Bridge of Pain	31
Gator	33
Nombre de Dios	35
St. Johns River	37
Barracks	39
Bartram Trail Incident	41
Lovers' Wall	43
Spanish Military Hospital	45

Characters Then and Now

Menendez	47
Tyler	49
Flagler	51
Charlie	53
Street People	54
Chieftain	55
Artisans	57
Timucua	59
Ghosts	61
Visitors	63

Things Not So Old

Carriage	67
San Sebastian Winery	69
Pier	71
Bunnery	73
Hog	75
Casa	77
Alligator Farm	79
Legion	81
Courtyard Café	83
Tour Train	85

Sense of Things

Early on St. George	89
Plaza	91
On the Beach Early	93
Imagine	95
St. George Street	97
Plaza Solace	99
Osprey	101
Old Town Thunderstorm	103
Calm Bay	105
The Other End	107
Place on the Bay	109
Finally	111

Ancient Places

Welcome

To capture the essence
of the Old Town, you
must look into her soul
for the stories
yet to be told,
waiting down the
narrow, worn streets
where the past
and you can meet
at places often passed
but not seen,
where you will
feel what it means
to enter the heart,
that beats to the echo
of hooves pulling a cart,
among whispers of the past
and things meant to last,
urging your imagination
be set free;
only then
will you truly see.

Ancient City

The Old Town is
not old at all
by some standards -
young, in the worldly
scheme of things.

But here, in this land,
it is the oldest.
Already a half-century old,
boasting a town with a
fort, shops, houses, when
those fleeing persecution
landed on that rock,
    further north.

Unique in that it is old
now, today, measured
by history, preserved in
places and rooms soaked
by smells and voices of times past,
    and more.

Downtown, Old Town, city proper,
where buildings are not so old,

but neither are they young,
even there, the aura of history,
the past, other times,
prevail.
You feel it. Sense it.
It enters you
with a mystique
in the air that
seems to rush down
the narrow streets.

"You have such a unique town,"
I have been told.
The intent to convey
something special,
something words alone
cannot do.

But I understand.
It entered them.
Adventures of times past.
Mystery, never ending.
Romance, past and present.
History still alive.
A glimpse of what was.

Aviles Street

Standing beneath
the ancient archway,
I am jealous
of the old cracking
stones,
of what they have
seen, heard.
I am alone here,
but not lonely;
the past shares
my solitude
as I seek
secrets stored
in these stones.
Moving down this,
the oldest of streets,
on rough, uneven
bricks, I watch
shadows dance
over the moonlit
old hospital
and reflect
on the volumes
about those

times in the
library further down
guarded by that society.
I can smell ghosts
as I move forward
to the past, and
I am jealous.

Tolomato

Tread softly
over this small tract,
be mindful of what it is,
what it holds within
hallowed ground.
The story of this place,
this oldest city,
is here,
in the ashes of
Guale, Timucua,
Spanish, English, slaves,
Minorcan . . . others.
Some notable,
some not.
Stand quietly.
Feel the centuries
course through your
mortal soul.
Listen for a sound,
search within for
a sign.

It is here,
with all these hundreds,
life extinguished into
the history that lives
in this place.

Oldest Drugstore

Through the street window
of that old store,
trapped by ancient
panes in wooden,
over-polished cabinets,
can be seen the
cure-alls dispensed by
Speissegger and Gomaas.
Castor oil. Rose water.
Chills and fever tonic.
St. Augustine's famous remedy
to prevent all manner of maladies.
Potent medicines, Indian herbs,
and if all else failed,
concoctions known
only to the apothecary,
mixed carefully with
mortar and pestle.
Potions, lotions, and remedies!

Old, wooden floors creak
under the weight of ghosts
inspecting dark bottles boasting
labels of cure and guarantee
in the lingering, antiseptic smell
permeating air thick with
wisps of the past.

Old Jail

Cold steel and brick camouflaged
by that wealthy railroad magnate
with stucco, in Queen Ann style.

Matching the playhouses of
rich friends on holiday, some
forsaking afternoon tennis to
hear the gallows' door thump.

No view through those barred windows.
Floors and walls blank,
causing memory and fantasy to merge.

Thoughts of escape
from that plank bed
and threadbare cover,

but failure would conjure
more indignities from
slow-witted, ungrateful guards.

Tasteless food and rusty water
to pamper what spirits left,
taken with emancipated reason,
Savored slowly over the
objections of visiting mice and
amusement of the spinning spider.

Old Town Streets

Giant, ancient trees
stand silently in
yards among
those old houses,
watching over ghosts
of gentlemen suitors
walking stiffly up
stone steps
to the sound of
music through
an open door
and the slow plodding
of a passing carriage.

Ghosts are walking.
Their movements cause
garden flowers
to rustle slightly
spreading a pleasant fragrance
through the air
surrounding mustached gentlemen
and refined ladies
strolling arm in arm
through the Old Town streets.

Castillo De San Marcos

The Castillo would not fall.
Coquina carefully laid, each wall;
cut from rock of sand and shell,
by peons in the island quarry that was hell,
    and the Castillo would not fall.

Pried from the island floor with timbers tall,
across that inlet they would haul;
pulling, tugging with calloused hands,
footprints left deep in hot sand,
    and the Castillo would not fall.

Bastioned, parts snaking from the main wall,
making each end tower appear small;
made so for lookouts to give the cry
if their flag the approaching ship did not fly,
    and the Castillo would not fall.

Some vibration, a thud, from cannon ball
hurled from ships to that wall,
once, relentless for thirty days,
'til that Brit sailed away on friendlier waves;
    and the Castillo would not fall.

Over centuries, many tried; Brits, Gauls,
to penetrate that bastioned wall;
pounding storms, driving rain,
tourists' footsteps, all the same,
   the Castillo will not fall.

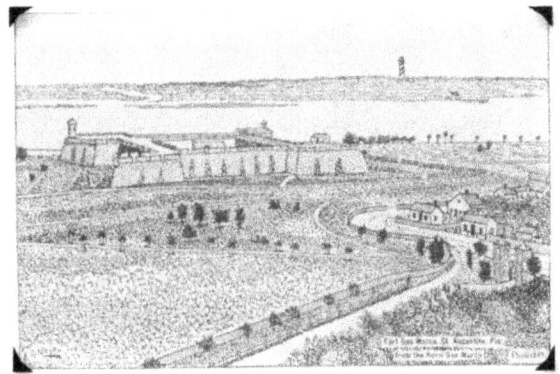

Lighthouse Porch

Early one morning while
seeking solitude on the
old lighthouse porch,
a pleasant sound
floated into my ear;
not yet dawn, only
distant sounds from
the inlet.
Quiet.
My reason for being here.

I searched among the trees,
still sparkling from dew
in the pale light, and finally,
as dawn gave way to day,
I glimpsed a small bird
just as it fluttered away,

and with it the song.
One lone branch, the stage,
like a conductor's wand
swayed to and fro;
happiness flown away.
And sorry was I
it chose to go.

Oldest House

I stoop to pass through
the modest doorway
and smell ghosts
of the artillery man
and feel the movement
of Mary's transient
guests.
Generations of Alvarez.
A glance at sparse
furnishings.
The tour guide's
voice is barely
audible.
For that is not what I want.
I want this room.
The sense of it,
rooted in a million
past footsteps.
I'm jealous
of what I cannot
see; hear.

Fulfilled dreams not witnessed.
But I feel it,
in the rock hard wood,
the air, full of life,
holding the past.

Lasting

Carriages
can't be replaced.
Trains came.
Busses came.
Taxis came.
Still, the horses
plod along, pulling the
　carriages,
at a snail's pace,
with aroma.
Not defiant
or humble.
　Just here.
　Everywhere.
　Plodding along.
Not necessary.
But then, neither
is the Fort or
that old Ponce place.
To pave over
nostalgic, old
brick or cobblestone
is . . . unthinkable.

So, too, is banishing
the carriages that fit
the narrow twists
and turns of those
streets, with the
banter of all that
is the Old Town.

Plaza Beginning

We can thank
that Spanish King
four centuries ago
for declaring La Florida
towns outward from
center plazas would go.

The hub of activity;
all manner of goods
brought in for sale
to eager buyers summoned
forth by the sound
of the King's bell.

From narrow,
cobbled streets,
they would heed the call,
passing under overhanging
balconies through the scent
of lush gardens behind
stone patio walls.

Even now it beckons
to all who come,
traversing worn streets
to the center
of all things old;
   the place to meet.

Renovation

What fascination we have
re-making the old houses
of the ancient city.
Workers treading cautiously
across thin planks supported
precariously by a woven
tangle of iron.
Blue gauze air, laces
of light bending through
ancient panes.
High, peaked ceilings with
the smells of times past,
Walls soaked with
residue from countless
cookings; blending
of food, burning wood, charcoal,
oil.
It's work. But love too.
Strong calves and thighs
flicker from constant
stooping, climbing.
Eyes sting from
sweat, slippery tools
hard to hold.

With the late sky
dimming through old
slatted vents, tired
workman snake down
the scaffolds like grey
spiders, carefully. No net.
A dangerous business,
re-making the old.
Preserving history.
With love.
Making old new;
  But old...

Oldest Schoolhouse

Were they here, now, those
   students of a time far away,
youth of the Old Town,
   what would they say?
Sequestered within these old walls,
tempted by the smell of the sea,
learning the alphabet, A to Z,
what did they see?
What could they tell me?

Scratching of pencils
   on slate boards again and again,
the swift rap on knuckles
   for the smallest sin
from a strict headmaster,
   where discipline was the rule
and for those daily hours,
   only one reigned; nobody's fool.

After the three "R's,"
   how many stayed in this place,
how many chose to leave
   with undue haste?
What stories of the Old Town
   would they tell me, or you,
of those times, this place;
   if only we knew.

Fountain of Youth

Keepers of that fountain
from which water flows freely
from the earth, clear and cool,
allude to its mystical power,
giver of eternal life.

For his king, Ponce, explorer
of small stature and large dreams,
claimed this land, this La Florida,
and sought the origin, and truth,
of the tale, then sailed away,

to return years later
to dislodge others and
continue the quest, but found
instead that crude, shell tipped
staff lodged deep into his body.

Three stately Spanish galleons
slicing through green waters
away from this land,
laden with its fruit, fresh meat,
and cool water, life ebbing slowly
from the conqueror.

Bridge Of Pain

That old bridge
graced by lions,
struggling against
pounding wheels,
the elements,
 and time.

The vague sea,
calmed somewhat
as the inlet
it has become creeps
further in,
nipping at the great
columns relentlessly,
year after year pushed
 by tide and wind.

Unchanged, save for
the seasonal follies
of man, when the
great spans are adorned
with first lights, then flags,
now banners;
 still the same.

Adored, even when
its rusty hinges
and grease filled
gears force open
its cavernous mouth
without shame
for that distant sail,
when it becomes the
   bridge of pain.

Gator

If the river has a king,
surely it is this beast

from another time,
defying evolution,

unchanged, gliding through
the centuries among lilies

and eel grass like
a roughly carved log

with two peering knots
that see all,

its giant form guided
by that sweet, deadly flesh,

washing waves over the
banks of his kingdom.

Nombre de Dios

I gaze up,
awestruck,
at the imposing
symbol of Christianity.
'Name of God'.
First mission
of this land.
I watch as it
slices the sun,
causing rays of
silver light to dance
before my eyes.
I sense ghosts
of holy water
where gentle men
went into the
wilderness with
its spirit,
unafraid.
I sense miracles
and I am humbled.

St. Johns River

Ancient river, now calm,
   at peace,
haven for all manner
   of fish, fowl, beast.
Cypress lined shores
   hedged with green,
movement among
   massive roots, unseen.
You reach into swamps
   flowing backward from south
among dense trees
   shielding the moccasin's
swift, white mouth;
   where gator backs
and logs blend,
   unfettered by northeast winds.
Masterpiece of sunsets
   reflecting over the
   vastness before me,
into the wetness,
each different,
so many more
will I never see.
Your lapping water

   tugs at my soul,
mixed with ancient chants,
   stories told and re-told,
around campfires
   of moss and stone
hidden below your surface
   among charred bone.
My course is fragile,
a ripple that fades away
   as I move on,
like so many before
who walked your banks
   and then were gone.
But you are permanent,
   flowing north, forever,
   into that vast ocean
   where your end
      is never.

Barracks

Before the Old
Town was so old,
in a time past,
when life was gentle,
the pace not so fast,
with the close
of each day,
near the south end
just off the bay,

on St. Francis Street,
the strollers would meet,

and in the last dance
of lingering shade
soldiers would march,
in full dress parade.

Townspeople and visitors
alike would stand
as cadence was called
to music from the barracks' band.

Reflections off brass
in the dimming light;
music, conversation, and laughter,
blending with the night.

Bartram Trail Incident

Just out of town
along the river,
on that trail, Bartram,
in l840, a traveling troupe,
under the moon, silver,
headed to a performance
in the Old Town,
encountered a band of hostiles,
wild from drink,
yelping strange sounds.

Educated thespians,
city bred,
not comprehending their plight,
found themselves dead
on that cool, pleasant night.
But justice would
soon prevail,
from the end of ropes
at the oldest jail.
It seems there was no
need for any to confess,
because the hostiles, you see,
came to town, and in
the troupe's costumes
they were dressed.

Lovers' Wall

Tourists note with
some relief when
walking our ancient seawall
that it is ample
in width, giving little
chance one might fall.

For this, it is young,
star struck Captain
Dancy we can thank,
creating that spacious
path along the gurgling
foam of the ocean's bank.

He did so
not from necessity
or some engineer's test,
but, rather, from a
need he felt that
two should walk abreast.

The captain, you see,
was in love,
struck hard by
the moon above,
and when strolling with
his lady along the tide,
he figured how neat it
would be to walk side by side.

Spanish Military Hospital

No blinking monitors,
I-V's, or nurse
call buttons here,
in this place where the
sight of crude instruments
could bring a tear.
Soldiers with some
malady, or perhaps
wound from a sword,
lay under the surgeon's
scrutiny on a
bed of board.
A place, no doubt,
they did not choose
to long tarry,
awaiting the herbs
and medicines of
the apothecary!

Characters Then and Now

Menendez

A smuggler once, not
unfamiliar with the inside of a jail,
but all was forgiven by a king
bent on conquest and seeing no
match for this admiral under sail.

Weary from too many campaigns, the
fire within barely burned,
but from the shores of that place,
that La Florida, his son had not returned.
Amidst hope, perhaps meant to be,
he looked again to his beloved sea.

Opposing flags on galleons dipping
through the cold, green water
atop sails strained by urgency
to be first arrived;
with pomp and circumstance
befitting the rituals of his land,
he stepped ashore, in fifteen sixty-five.

The smuggler-turned-governor
and Captain General placed
a cross for his king,
and recalling his beloved Aviles
proclaimed this place after
its patron saint - Augustine.

PEDRO MENENDEZ DE AVILES
Founder of St. Augustine, Fla.

Tyler

On a clear, calm night
in the Old Town bay,
Tyler, made listless by the rum,

stumbled to the deck
and reached up to
the stars.

They were beyond his grasp,
and leaning, he fell
into the waiting arms
of the moon's lover

shattering the mirror surface.
Just as it reassembled,
Tyler emerged, mind forcing
his hand toward the deck rail

while his heart begged him
stay in the warm, liquid
arms, but

too late, the rail in his
grasp, the rum beckoning.

Flagler

Second founder of Old Town,
builder of that railway
snaking down the
coast through towns and
marshland, along the
scenic, green wetness, bringing
his guests to a skyline
kin to Old Spain.
To the first of those
great hotels: Ponce de Leon.
A coquina fortress
formed, not joined
with that native stone
under terra cotta
boasting domes
and spiral steeples
that stood watch
over gala balls
and elaborate picnics
of northern escapees.

Charlie

Weathered, worn face,
bulbous nose, ragged
mouth fixed in a
perpetual grin
  above a sunken chin.
Eyes laced with
red-worn,
under a furrowed brow
that resembles
a gathering storm.
  Charlie.
Asking for change
but somehow not begging,
and if none offered,
a shrug, then on to the next.
Watching tourists with
a reflective gaze,
perhaps seeing fond
memories through the haze,
or wondering where they
went, the better days.
Charlie...

Street People

The morning sun
causes a stir
from bodies in
sleeping bags or
curled in question
marks with old blankets.
St. Francis House full,
with these few scattered
about left to their
own devices; to rest, survive,
return from the night's high.

No answers, only questions.
Another day consigned
to unfulfillment.
One certainty for the
moment; stay close,
for breakfast is nigh.

Chieftain

Proud chief, unbowed,
rocked with the fever
   of his land,

but unconquered.

Brought to that great
fort of stone
   by trickery.

No treacherous general
could win the fight,
even with the great
Chieftain wilting in that
   small, damp room.

Dying in a different
land, far away,
on his terms,
   painted.

Still, no treaty.

Body among the worms,
headless. His presence
felt even now on moonlight
nights among the
   stacked coquina.

Great Chieftain forever.

Whose griefs were many.
Whose trust was betrayed.
Whose waters still flow.
Whose land and people,
   still free.

Artisans

The Old Town
is,
among other things,

a home to
artisans.
some notable,
  most self proclaimed.

Its quaint streets
and festive
(though with demeanor)
atmosphere lulls
  the writer, artist,
  the free thinking
  into secure warmth.

All others,
those visitors
treading into this
  delicate, imperfect world,
are but a necessity
required to cheer
the artisan,
without thought,
unaware of the wealth
  they have found.

Timucua

They were many.
Large, tawny bodies
bare, save for brief
patches of moss or
soft deerskin.
Adorned with simple
treasures of the land;
strings of polished pearls,
fish teeth bracelets,
brass ornaments that
tinkled with movement.
Tattoos signifying their place.
Sharing all things, taken
from the land with care,
with thanks given in
ceremony.
Sitting at day's end
around smoldering fires
under giant live oaks,
still in the coming darkness
with sleeping eyes, folded wings.
They were many.

The wind they worshipped
brought tall ships, blocking
their sun god's view.
Their words, strung together
like polished shells in patterns
passed on, father to son
became strange sounds
uttered by intruders.
Mystical names of the land
became as the others, recorded
like so much livestock.
Long, raven hair piled
high to taunt would-be
scalpers fell to the ground
with the great trees cut
to change villages to towns,
protected by a cross.
Then, there were none.

Ghosts

It is said there
are ghosts
in the Old Town.
Running amuck in
that old cemetery,
tipping ale in taverns,
pacing the floors of inns,
their spirits abound.
You may be a skeptic
or you may believe,
but for those wandering souls,
do not grieve;

enjoy their play
when you arrive,
those forms without faces,
keeping history alive
in all the old places.
And should you hear a noise
in that old house,
don't be alarmed,
it's probably just a mouse
scurrying away, causing
a creak in the wooden floor
and a moaning of old hinges
from the slowly closing door,
blocking your exit temporarily,
or perhaps, forevermore.

Visitors

The gaggle in the Plaza.

Most wandering aimlessly,
but some with a sense of purpose,
though known only to them.

Baggie shorts, sunglasses,
tanned legs, maps held
tightly, giving meaning to
an otherwise uncertain stroll.

Stops at intersections, map
orientation; discussion,
disagreement, decision,
then onward, hurriedly,
lest that next site, in place
for centuries, be gone.

THE GREASY POLE, CHRISTMAS, 1876,
ST. AUGUSTINE, FLA.

E. A. MEYER AT THE TOP

Corridor in the Public Library, Hospital Street, (now Aviles) St. Augustine, Fla.

Things Not So Old

Carriage

Starting you is
not always easy;
harder on a cold day;
reluctant, leaving a
warm barn and sweet hay.

Once brushed, braced,
and hitched, your single
desire is to return here;
to that end, you
are always slightly in gear.

Your load, on wheels
of wood and steel, roll
freely on these hard streets,
though you abhor stopping
where two meet.
Your brakes are marginal,
in a perpetual state
of the near miss,
due in part to a
foggy state of bliss.

Your ears are immune
to the constant banter
of the driver guide
imparting old city history
to those along for the ride.

Others from behind press impatiently
from their steel steed, but
to no avail, for you only
have one speed; until
of course, the barn is in sight,
then those reins must be
pulled ever so tight.

San Sebastian Winery

A dream born from
memories of a father's
homemade wine;
the lure of vineyards bursting
with fruit of the vine.

Soon, just over the inlet,
out of that old railway
building bordered by King
grew the San Sebastian winery
in the Old Town, St. Augustine.

Upon entering, a
happy, festive place
you will find,
among well appointed gifts
and tastings of
that grape, muscadine.

An open invitation
to sample the wares
or just bask in the sun
with great music upstairs.

Celebrations of harvest,
when festivals are held,
a visit to the past,
grape stomping
in authentic oaken barrels;

culinary delights,
and local art,
a gift to the Ancient City
given from the heart.

A refined place, yet folksy,
where laughter abounds.
A perfect fit, a dream realized,
nestled in the Old Town.

The Pier

Just past the lions
guarding that old bridge,
beyond that farm of gators,
under the tall palms
in the scent of the ocean,
there's a gathering;
Wednesday.
Every week, year 'round.
Just off the pier,
mixed with the scent
of salt air and pigeons
competing for dropped
morsels, the people come.
From all over.
All ages.
Locals. Vacationers. Passersby.

To this place of fresh
fruit and vegetables, arts, crafts,
crab cakes.
The pier; the market. The
   meeting place.
Different things for different people.
Tastes to suit all.
The buzz of relaxed conversation,
laughter, bartering, the occasional
posturing by canines tugging at
leashes to get a better
whiff of one of their own.
Sights, sounds, smells of life. . .
   of the pier.

The Bunnery

Smells that bring
life to my nose,
alerting taste buds
of things to come,

good things,
risen with care
from dough
kneaded gently

served hot with
butter skating across
toasted surface

and laced with
sweet, savory icing,
melting on
tongues unbelieving,

savored slowly,
with the buzz
and laughter of
friendly conversation

heard from St. George,
enticing others,
following the smell,
yielding to senses
urging enter, enter.

Hog

It's a happening
every year.
Like clockwork.
Just before new
buds grace the foliage
in the plaza.
Still a nip in the air.
But sunny.
A different breed,
on different steeds,
jarring the quiet,
breaking tourists' monotony
with a different sight.
Bandana's, levi's, leather;
four
or more,
to a space, kickstands
their tether.
Hogs that roar
instead of squeal,
high octane their meal.

Tolerated, even as old
town buildings shake,
middle-aged tourists thinking
that's where I'd like to be;
on a hog,
in the Old Town,
free.

Casa . . .

People watching
is a matter of location
in the Old Town.
For those who partake,
many places abound.

Several locations
come to mind,
some obvious,
some hard to find.

Filling the criteria
to see who's who,
and a great cup
of warm brew

is a place of which
I am particularly fond,
right across from
that dancing, concrete pond.

You can sit east or
west on its ornamental chairs
while others dwell within,
up and down
thickly carpeted stairs.

Wonderful snacks, served
by ladies with accents.
Check it out, after Flagler,
you'll be glad you went.

Alligator Farm

I am Tarzan.
This path of boards
under my feet is
not there,
for I am swinging
on ropes of vines
over the large gator jaws,
open,
snapping, as huge
tails thrash wildly,
sending waves across
the jungle moat.

In this place
where birds flash
bright colors
through giant green
tropical leaves,
and snakes through
slit eyes follow
my every movement;

where Gomek roamed
I am king;
for the moment,
in this zoological
park, this alligator
farm-this jungle.
It is all mine,
because, you see,
I am only nine!

Legion

One Anderson Circle,
overlooking the bay,
   they gather.

Teetering on stools
too wobbly for the unsteady,
but nothing more is offered
to these stout of heart,
these warriors of old
who have only their
   tales to be told.

Years change the
   events
or perhaps only the telling.
Stories are heard often by
those in frequent attendance.
No one seems to mind.

Cracked walls match
faces
that reflect years unkind,
and history understood
only by them.

War was youth
and dreams, but
now only blurred memories.

Talk is loud,
jokes are plentiful,
and on us.

Courtyard Cafe

A quaint unassuming
place, sharing tranquil days
with colorful flowers,
bright tropical plants;
a bridge of stone
that adorns a singing
pool alive with
shimmering Koi,
eyes fixed upward
to hopefully generous patrons
crossing the garden path.
In this ancient garden
in the shadows of Flagler's old Spain
architecture of stone and steeple,
where museums, shops, and offices
have replaced hotel parlors
and drawing rooms,
is a different place.
Step out of the bustling crowd
into a haven in the shade,
with a gentle breeze,
or the music of falling rain
on terra cotta;
the serenity of the courtyard,

meeting place of the rich
in times past-now yours,
to be savored with the
aroma of coffee and food
befitting this special place
you have discovered.

Tour Train

The caterpillar-like body
of the long sightseeing
train snakes around the
corner, laden with stickered
tourist gypsies, home now the
motel or bed and breakfast
where the rental car is parked.
Where clean shirts, road maps,
and coolers await.
Riders disembark to take in
the next site.
Harried mothers usher kids
away from the beast before it
crawls away.
Fathers in baggy shorts, paled
forever by the office left behind,
follow; glassy-eyed, stroller weary,
walking patiently,
lost behind plaza sunglasses
and tourist guide books,

dazed, anonymous faces unmoving
as the clanging bell of
the departing train jostles them
back to the task at hand.
Back to the melting ice cream and corndogs.
Back to the sights to behold.

Hospital Street, now Aviles Street, looking north, St. Augustine, Fla.

Sense of Things

Early On St. George

I walked alone down
St. George Street early,
before
dawn and the opening
of shop doors
   and heard soft voices
   mixed with the clank
   of armor and clopping
   of hooves on cobblestone;
and passed on,
with the sound lodged
   in my head.

ST. GEORGE STREET, ST. AUGUSTINE, FLORIDA
LOOKING NORTH FROM CATHEDRAL STREET

Plaza

It's friendly
in the Plaza.
Inviting.
Even hawking hustlers
are intriguing;
all have stories --
Some are even true.

Always in motion,
but at ease,
like the squirrels
and birds moving
over branches and
through the air.

Each scene, daily,
different. Caused so
by changing faces;
some to never return,
just as a fallen leaf
cannot lift itself
to join the twig once again.

Perhaps that is the why
for friendly chatter
between strangers;
sharing this place,
this time,
with the fragility
of an unbruised flower.

On The Beach Early

Walking this desolate
beach early, to
only the sound of
purity; sandpipers
and gulls feeding among
the gentle swells,
inattentive, for I
alone am here
with them and share
their brief respite.

With the solitude, head
and heart venture
into reconciliation,
perhaps understanding.

Water foams beneath
my feet, completing its
journey, my own
still unfolding.

As the pattern of water
shore bound breaks around
my ankles I feel
sadness,
for I am the intruder.

With the sun I
must leave this
beach, before my
head fills with
portentous pettiness
that is a part of my
journey but has no
place here.

Imagine

I have discovered
on some Old Town streets,
those fronting ancient
shops and houses,
where bricks and cobblestone meet,

against a misty dawn,
one can imagine sights
and sounds of times past
before manicured lawns.

Emerging from ornate houses,
well-brushed, mustached gentlemen
in stiff white collars
off to their shops.

Snorting, morning sounds
of an old horse, withers
trembling, warming to
the day's work.

The smell of smoke
on the bay front,
rising from an old barrel
warming boat workers
huddled amongst great pilings,
surrounded by shrieking gulls.

The haunting sound
of a foghorn,
announcing the start
of another day's ritual,
echoing through
the small streets and
alleys of the Old Town.

St. George Street

Every tourist who enters
the Old Town gates
will eventually stroll
St. George Street.

They are of every size and description.

Preserving the poetry of diversity.

Persistent,
moving ever forward,
an integral part of the
caterpillar that is this
mass of humanity.

Pigeons move deftly
among feet,
unscathed
by the sweat of
tightly packed captives.

Street smells.
Chocolate.
Displays announcing
every souvenir possible.

New mixed with
old; blending.
Alive.

Plaza Solace

Solace is temporary
in the Plaza
but worth even
a brief respite.
Be aloof to the
street sellers;
glance instead
at birds dancing
in circles, converging,
chasing, then flying
away, disappearing
into the sky.
The hustlers will think
you strange and
move, mumbling, to
other targets,
leaving you with
your bench and
nuts for the squirrels.

Osprey

Exquisitely graceful flight,
floating, far up
in that gray area,
surveying the warm
map of the land
through seams
only they see.
Diving, wings tucked,
through a core in space,
swift and straight,
delivery strict, classic,
with talons reversed,
transformed to razors
that strike deep into
unsuspecting prey,
lifted up by powerful
six-foot wings,
carried away to another,
perched atop a giant cone
of branches and moss.

Always two.
A permanent presence,
mated for life,
working in tandem.
Raptors,
beauty, pure expertise.

Old Town Thunderstorm

On hot, humid
August days
it comes.
Now, rumbling from above,
below,
trapped between old buildings
and trembling
brick streets,
causing youngsters to
shiver and cling
tightly to nervous legs.
Slash of power,
bright against a dark
sky as lightning
cracks, forcing squeals
and nervous comments
from tourists in limbo.

The rain, in a gush,
comes, strong, powerful,
deafening to those lucky ones
huddled in the
ancient structures, anxious.
Be not afraid.
This aged lumber and stone
has sheltered many others,
through many years
and many storms.

The Calm Bay

Nothing feels more calm
than the small vastness
of the bay between Marine Street
and the 'island' on a
hot, humid, still summer night.
After the afternoon breezes
have yielded to twilight and darkness.

The tourist traffic gone,
soaking tired feet,
or enjoying Old Town cuisine
further up.
Alone, sitting on the wall
separating wetness from pavement.
No crickets here, gulls gone-sleeping.
No lapping sounds, for the tide is
awaiting change; still, not yet ready
to move in or out.

Dim lights from the floating
homes of the boat people.
Not twinkling from the water movement
because it is, for brief moments,
unmoving, resisting the pull of

a scarred moon that enhances the calmness.
No warm breeze to dry my sweat.

The tradeoff for this stillness as
I listen to voices from out there,
from the boats anchored
in the darkness;
the sounds in my ears
allowed to linger by the
absent wind.

Now, in this place, at this time,
I am both secure and in awe
because I know, at any moment, at
another time the power of a
storm will change all this, or the
tide will begin its movement.
The lights will move, mixed
with the clanking of boat bells
and moaning of anchor ropes.
Then I will move on,
for it will not be the same.

The Other End

I know a place
tucked away,
  secret.

Off the beaten path,
the opposite end of St. George,
 isolated.

Here, one can find quiet,
out of the hustle and bustle;
  solitude.

Shaded, calm.
benches for rest,
  or reflection.

An unkempt old well
for your wishes,
  or secrets.

Next to that old inn.
the other end of St. George;
  secret...

Old Don Toledo House, Aviles Street, St. Augustine, Fla.

A Place On The Bay

Leave the gift shops,
street hustlers and
trolleys for a change of scene
down by the bay,
a calmer place,
natural, serene.

Find that place
south of the fish feeding
restaurant--as far
as you can stroll
that way.

Your choice of seawall
or grass;
sit among the old stone.
Watch the lights fade.
Hear the inlet murmurs.
Feel the sea wind.

With the last light
of evening,
when washing sea sounds
become a gurgle,
you'll be happy you
sought out this place.

Finally

Enjoy the Old Town
in early morning
before you depart.
When her narrow streets
are unburdened by
the weight of steel beasts,
and the only sounds
are your footsteps,
echoing in small
caverns between old,
worn walls.
Without the distraction
of trolley bells and
tour guide narrative.
With only your thoughts,
your imagination.
Wander without
benefit of maps
and brochures.
Let the mystique
enter you and follow
your soul.

About the Author

Randy Cribbs, a native of Florida, is a 2005 Much Ado About Books featured author who has become an increasingly popular and productive author. Six books have been published in the past three years. His latest novel, "The Vessel", an Ancient City mystery, was published in the fall of 2005. A graduate of the FBI Academy and the Armed Forces Staff College, he holds degrees from the University of Florida, Pacific Lutheran University, and Jacksonville State University. He resides in St. Augustine, Florida, where he teaches and writes.

Also by Randy Cribbs:

The Vessel

When the body of archaeologist William Stewart is found floating in the bay, Robert Robson finds himself caught up in a web of hideous secrets, deceit and murder woven by the lure of the tinaja and its terrifying power.

At first, his empirical mind refuses to believe the old Indian story, but as he is drawn deeper into Stewart's past, each ghastly revelation points to an unimaginable power and moves him dangerously close to the line that separates right from wrong, fact from myth; and now, that power may be within his grasp . . .

ISBN 0-9725796-4-8 Paperback 224 pages

Tales from the Oldest City

The author's affection for the nation's oldest city and old Florida is evident is this colorful collection of short stories.

From the mystery of "So Little Time" and adventure of "Mike's Birds" to the heartwarming "Riverman" and humor of "Peanuts", readers are presented with a broad variety of tales guaranteed to tickle the imagination.

Randy's ability to blend fact and fiction into entertaining stories makes this picturesque tour through the Old Town a special way to visit and revisit the unique places, history, and colorful characters of St. Augustine, the St. Johns River, and surrounding area.

ISBN 0-9725796-1-3   Paperback   160 pages

One Summer in the Old Town

The author's first novel draws the reader into a summer adventure set in St. Augustine and on the St. Johns River. A well-researched, historical overview of the nation's oldest city is woven into the fast paced story through a host of colorful characters

"One Summer in the Old Town" is a great story and

an interesting, fun way to learn about the history, landmarks, and mystique of the Old Town.

Used by schools and book clubs throughout the region, this book is enjoyed by all ages. Includes original pen and ink drawings by artist, Manila Clough.
ISBN 0-9725796-2-1 Paperback 160 pages

Illumination Rounds

The gripping cover suggests more than just war stories-and it is much more. Co-authored with award winning journalist Peter Guinta, these stories are mystery, romance, adventure, drama, and humor. They present a graphic portrayal of American soldiers and marines who served in Vietnam.

Both authors draw from personal experiences, blending fact and fiction into a captivating before, during, and after picture of the men who fought. Their styles and recollections complement each other to capture the tragedy, humor, and perspective of the young men in that controversial conflict, but the understanding goes beyond the 'Vietnam experience' to today's citizens, family, and friends of the young men and women who are America's warriors around the world.
ISBN 0-9725796-4-8 Paperback 196 pages

Were You There: Vietnam Notes

Everything in the author's memory of Vietnam comes alive in his poetry: times of fear and love, moments of realization, the landscape, and the soldiers.

Presented in sections, the poems and supporting illustrations by Matt Cribbs take the reader to the place, shows the people, describes 'the job', 'things' in our head', and looks in the 'duffel bag' and its humor.

"'Were You There' reflects a deep understanding of war, those who go to fight and their families. Every bit as appropriate today as it was then."

Schools, groups, as well as friends and families of today's young men and women serving in the Armed Forces applaud 'Were You There' as a tool of understanding, appreciation, and perspective of those in harm's way.

ISBN 0-9725796-0-5 Paperback 160 pages

For more information go to:
www.somestillserve.com

www.ingramcontent.com/pod-product-compliance
Lightning Source LLC
Chambersburg PA
CBHW051450290426
44109CB00016B/1700